CW01652665

Fl... ...se Pocketbook

AS/A-Level Physical Education

Historical Factors & Contemporary Issues

Philip Allan Updates, an imprint of Hodder Education, an Hachette UK company, Market Place, Deddington, Oxfordshire OX15 0SE

Orders

Bookpoint Ltd, 130 Milton Park, Abingdon, Oxfordshire OX14 4SB
tel: 01235 827720 fax: 01235 400454 e-mail: uk.orders@bookpoint.co.uk

Lines are open 9.00 a.m.–5.00 p.m., Monday to Saturday, with a 24-hour message answering service. You can also order through our website: www.philipallan.co.uk

ISBN 978-1-4441-1544-4

First printed 2010

Impression number 5 4 3 2 1
Year 2014 2013 2012 2011 2010

Printed in Spain

P01743

Historical Factors

1 Popular recreation I
2 Popular recreation II
3 Popular recreation III
4 Social revolutions
5 Industrial Revolution
6 Leisure
7 Rational recreation
8 Religion
9 Muscular Christianity
10 Youth movement
11 Working class
12 Middle class
13 Upper class
14 Hanoverian era
15 Victorian era
16 Edwardian era
17 Interwar years (1918–39) I
18 Interwar years (1918–39) II
19 1939–45 and postwar Britain
20 Government intervention
21 Influential characters
22 Amateurism I
23 Amateurism II
24 Amateurism III
25 Professionalism
26 Professional sport
27 Social reforms
28 British Empire
29 Olympism
30 Public school I
31 Public school II
32 Girls' public school
33 Proprietary college
34 Athleticism
35 University
36 Governing body
37 State school
38 Swedish Gymnastics
39 Model Course
40 Syllabuses of physical training
41 Movement approach
42 *Moving and Growing*
43 Teaching style
44 Blood sport
45 Swimming
46 Racket sports
47 Team games
48 Outdoor activity
49 Individual activities I
50 Individual activities II

Contemporary Issues

Popular recreation I

Q1 Which social class was most involved in popular recreation?

Q2 What football game was an example of popular recreation?

Q3 Give three characteristics of popular recreation.

Q4 Why did popular recreation decline?

ANSWERS

recreational pursuits with limited structure, which were fashionable before the Industrial Revolution

A1 Working class/lower class/peasantry

A2 Mob football

A3 Choose from: played occasionally; few rules; used force rather than skill; played by lower classes; local rather than national; limited structure and equipment; participation-based; violent (due to few rules); alcohol-fuelled

A4 Disapproval of middle/upper classes; need for a disciplined workforce; damage to property in towns; social control; lack of space; some activities were banned by law (e.g. mob football and blood sports)

***examiner's* note** Recreational pastimes reflect the lifestyles of a population and are subject to change as society develops. Popular recreation was enjoyed mainly by the lower classes, reflecting their lifestyle of limited leisure time, low income and little or no education.

Popular recreation II

Q1 How did mob football reflect the lifestyle of an agricultural worker?

Q2 Many rural sports took place on h.................. days.

Q3 The H.................. Games is a traditional festival that emerged in Scottish society and is famous for activities such as tossing the caber.

Q4 Name two recreational activities that owe their origin to rivers.

ANSWERS

recreational pursuits with limited structure, which were fashionable before the Industrial Revolution

A1 Played occasionally (on holy days/festivals); no written rules as players were not educated; brutal and harsh; simple equipment, as players had no money

A2 Holy

A3 Highland

A4 Choose from: swimming; rowing; fishing; ice skating

***examiner's* note** The recreational pastimes of a population reflect social changes and are subject to change as society develops.

Popular recreation III

Q1 M........ W........ O........ Games was a festival established in 1850 by Dr William Penny Brookes.

Q2 The C........ Games was an annual sports event that was revived by Robert Dover and became known as the Dover Games.

Q3 Why did many rural activities decline or disappear?

Q4 Why did some rural activities, such as the Highland Games in Scotland, survive?

ANSWERS

recreational pursuits with limited structure, which were fashionable before the Industrial Revolution

A1 Much Wenlock Olympian

A2 Cotswold

A3 The population became predominantly urban; limited space; different values needed for a disciplined workforce; some rural sports were banned by the middle/upper classes, e.g. mob football

A4 Less open to outside influences, owing to geographical isolation, so traditions easier to maintain; helped provide a cultural identity

***examiner's* note** Many activities developed as a functional need. When that need no longer existed, the activities often survived as recreational pursuits.

Social revolutions

Q1 The A.................. Revolution signified a change in farming practices that resulted in people moving to towns to seek work.

Q2 The I.................. Revolution resulted in the British economy changing from a largely agricultural one to one dominated by manufacturing.

Q3 The U.................. Revolution was a consequence of industrialisation as a vast body of people moved to towns to seek employment.

Q4 What effect did industrialisation have on the recreational pastimes of the working classes?

ANSWERS

far-reaching and drastic changes in society, especially in ideas and methods

A1 Agrarian

A2 Industrial

A3 Urban

A4 Less space for traditional pastimes such as mob football; less leisure time owing to long working days; less income for leisure; less energy due to poor health

***examiner's* note** The movement into towns initially led to a decline in recreational activities for the working classes due to long working hours, poor conditions of work, low pay, cramped housing and poor health. Towards the end of the nineteenth century, conditions began to improve. Working hours were reduced, wages began to rise and recreational opportunities gradually increased.

Industrial Revolution

Q1 Approximately how many years did the Industrial Revolution take?

Q2 What effect did urbanisation have on activities such as mob football?

Q3 What effect did the railways have on a variety of sports?

Q4 Which social class emerged as a result of the Industrial Revolution and became the controllers and administrators of sport?

ANSWERS

the process in the eighteenth and nineteenth centuries when the British economy changed from being primarily agricultural to being dominated by manufacturing

A1 100 years, from 1750 to 1850

A2 Lack of space; had to be banned for fear of damage to property

A3 Allowed day trips to the seaside; access to countryside increased participation in sports such as fishing, mountaineering, rambling and cycling; games like football could become regional and national; animals (such as horses) could be transported more easily

A4 Middle class

***examiner's* note** You need to understand how recreational pastimes reflect the lifestyles of a population.

Leisure

Q1 Give three reasons to account for the type of leisure the upper classes enjoyed in the nineteenth century.

Q2 Why did industrialisation initially lead to a decline in recreational opportunities for the working classes?

Q3 How did conditions improve for the working classes with respect to recreational opportunities?

Q4 In what ways were working hours reduced for the working classes in the late nineteenth century?

ANSWERS

time when there is an element of freedom for the individual to choose what to do

A1 Choose from: had plenty of free time; had a lot of money; could afford costly equipment/facilities; gambled on outcomes of events; often acted as patrons for lower-class performers

A2 Long working week; Sunday, the only day of rest, was kept free for church; no free daylight hours in winter; low pay

A3 Working hours began to be reduced; factory owners promoted sport for their workers via sponsored teams and day excursions

A4 Factory Acts; half-day Saturday; Bank Holiday Act 1871; early closing Wednesday

***examiner's* note** The recreational activities of the different social classes reflected their lifestyles.

Rational recreation

Q1 Rational recreation replaced p.................. recreation.

Q2 R.................. tennis was one of the earliest examples of rational recreation.

Q3 Give three characteristics of rational recreation.

Q4 Why was rational recreation used as a form of social control?

ANSWERS

A1 Popular

A2 Real

A3 Choose from: undertaken regularly; complex, written rules; highly structured; spectator-based; refined skills; developed by middle and upper classes; sophisticated equipment and facilities

A4 The middle and upper social classes wanted to control the recreational habits of the working classes; requirement for a civilised population with orderly working habits; rational sport helped to develop 'moral values'

***examiner's* note** Rational recreation was created by the upper/middle classes, reflecting their privileged lifestyle, which was characterised by ample leisure time, high income and good education.

Religion

Q1 The P............... work ethic held that recreational pursuits were a waste of time.

Q2 What effect did the evangelists have on the recreation time of the working classes in the nineteenth century?

Q3 How did the Sabbatarians influence the participation of the working classes in sporting activities?

Q4 The M............... associated recreation with alcohol, gambling and sin.

ANSWERS ❯❯

A1 Protestant

A2 Restrictive; they believed that popular recreation was sinful and associated it with gambling and alcohol

A3 They strongly disapproved of leisure activities on Sundays — the only day free from work for the working classes

A4 Methodists

***examiner's* note** The attitudes of most religious denominations in the nineteenth century restricted the recreational opportunities of the working classes, since these were believed to be a sinful waste of time and associated with gambling and alcohol. Religion was a major form of social control. The upper classes could afford to observe the Sabbath as they had plenty of leisure time during the week.

Muscular Christianity

Q1 Explain Muscular Christianity in terms of sport.

Q2 Explain athleticism in terms of sport.

Q3 Why did the Muscular Christians encourage athletic activities?

Q4 What influence did the YMCA have on sporting activities?

ANSWERS

an evangelical movement combining the Christian and chivalric ideals of manliness

A1 Ethical values; working for a team; conforming to rules; principles of fair play/sportsmanship; playing honourably is more important than winning; use of God-given talents; performance dedicated to God

A2 Physical endeavour with moral integrity; manliness; devotion to the physical; appreciation of values of a healthy lifestyle; accepting discipline of rational and rule-regulated activity

A3 Belief that healthy bodies were needed alongside healthy minds; form of social control; moral element

A4 Development of Christian ideals through group activities; spread sport via urban centres; invented volleyball and basketball

***examiner's* note** Athleticism and Muscular Christianity both involved the belief that the moral aspects were as important as the physical benefits.

Youth movement

Q1 Why did the Church become more positive about recreational pursuits for the working classes later in the nineteenth century?

Q2 What does YMCA stand for? What role did this organisation play in the development of the game of basketball?

Q3 How did the Church encourage recreational activities for parishioners?

Q4 Why were youth movements such as the Boys' Brigade and the Scouts encouraged by the Church?

ANSWERS

an organisation providing leisure activities for young people; often associated with a church

A1 Recruitment to church; recreational activities had become more rational and had moral values associated with them

A2 Young Men's Christian Association; Dr James Naismith invented the game to occupy and channel the energies of young men

A3 Provided facilities such as church halls; established clubs, e.g. Aston Villa; Sunday-school teams; youth movements, such as the Boys' Brigade

A4 Religious belief; helped promote moral and militaristic values; instilled social control; provided opportunities for outdoor activity

***examiner's* note** Military and moral values were encouraged through participation in physical activities.

Working class

Q1 Why did working-class women have the fewest recreational opportunities in nineteenth century society?

Q2 What other terms have been used to describe the working classes?

Q3 Why was compulsory schooling initially unpopular with the working classes?

Q4 What type of physical activities were taught in state schools in the nineteenth century and why?

ANSWERS

a social class occupied mainly by manual labourers

A1 Had less money, leisure time and power and fewer rights

A2 Peasants; lower classes; commoners

A3 Working-class families lost a source of income, as children used to work; working-class people disliked the controlling influence of the government/middle-class people

A4 Military drill and Swedish Gymnastics; required no facilities or equipment; could cater for large numbers in a small space; prepared the working classes for work and war; developed fitness and obedience

***examiner's* note** The working classes had little control in society until they became organised and developed as a force the authorities had to reckon with. Their conditions of work and lifestyles gradually improved with increasing public provision of facilities.

Middle class

Q1 What effect did the middle classes have on sport and recreation in the nineteenth century?

Q2 What was the role of middle-class women in the late nineteenth century?

Q3 Why was lawn tennis considered suitable for middle- and upper-class ladies to play?

Q4 What social revolution resulted in the emergence of the middle classes?

ANSWERS

a social class usually associated with non-manual, professional occupations

A1 Civilising and moral force due to strict religious observance; bans on blood sports; administrators of sport via governing bodies; codified sports and established sporting competitions; became managers and promoters

A2 Became professionals, such as teachers and nurses; fought for women's rights; established a more valuable education for girls

A3 Played in private gardens or clubs; rational activity; non-contact; could be played with men; could play in long dresses

A4 Industrial Revolution

***examiner's* note** The middle classes emerged from the Industrial Revolution. They aspired to the upper-class lifestyle and wished to disassociate themselves from the lower classes. They became the administrators and moral force in the world of sport.

Upper class

Q1 What other terms are used to signify the upper classes?

Q2 What privileges did the gentry enjoy in terms of lifestyle in the nineteenth century?

Q3 Members of the upper classes often took the role of a patron. What did this involve?

Q4 R.................. t.................. was one of the earliest forms of rational recreation for the upper classes.

ANSWERS

a social class comprising aristocratic families who held power and passed their titles to their heirs

A1 Aristocracy; nobility; gentry (note: *not* middle class)

A2 Wealth; plenty of leisure time; prestigious education; varied recreational opportunities

A3 Sponsoring an athlete from private funds; the athlete would then perform for the honour of the patron

A4 Real tennis

examiner's note The Industrial Revolution weakened the position of the upper classes as new wealth was created and traditional methods of gaining money from tenant farmers started to wane. Because upper-class people believed in the need for breeding and social status, they tried to avoid contact with the middle classes.

Hanoverian era

Q1 Over approximately how many years did the Industrial Revolution occur? (a) 50 (b) 75 (c) 100

Q2 What were the significant economic changes that occurred as a result of the Industrial Revolution?

Q3 How did the recreational pastimes of the working classes change as a result of the Industrial Revolution?

Q4 What was the influence on sports of the British Empire?

ANSWERS

the period of time relating to the monarchs of England reigning from 1714 to 1901

A1 (c) 100 (approximately 1750–1850)

A2 New wealth as a result of trade; manufacturing on a mass scale; working classes began to have higher disposable income; middle classes began to form the bourgeoisie; commercialisation became more important

A3 Lack of space for activities such as mob football; long working hours meant less time for recreational activities; activities became more rational and rule-based; cruel blood sports banned

A4 Britain spread its own sports, e.g. cricket, across the world and imported sports, e.g. polo, from other countries; the British system of sports clubs spread across the world

***examiner's* note** It is important that you understand historical terminology, such as 'late nineteenth century' and 'early twentieth century'.

Victorian era (1837–1901)

Q1 The Victorian era was a period of social reform. What were the intentions of the numerous Factory Acts during this time?

Q2 What were the motives behind the provision of parks in the nineteenth century?

Q3 What influence did the railways have on recreational opportunities for the working classes in the nineteenth century?

Q4 How did inns/pubs influence recreational opportunities?

ANSWERS

A1 To reduce working hours and improve working conditions for the working classes

A2 To improve health; to discourage crime; alternative to the pub; opportunities for recreational activities; to boost prestige of towns

A3 Transportation of spectators; fixtures became more frequent, regional, national and international; access to the countryside for rambling and cycling; factory owners put on seaside excursions for workers

A4 Games such as fives, rackets, boxing and quoits were encouraged; cricket teams would use field next to pub; liquor tents were provided by publicans at sporting events; football teams often associated with pubs

examiner's note The Victorian era saw the birth of modern sport.

Edwardian era (1901–10)

Q1 What factors caused organised sport to expand rapidly during the Edwardian period?

Q2 Why were sports such as golf and tennis still the preserve of the middle and upper classes?

Q3 Why did professional football increase its influence during the Edwardian period?

Q4 What activities were state schools offering working-class children during the Edwardian period?

ANSWERS

A1 Increased leisure time; better transport; increasing influence of media; developments in technology; communications; consolidation of sports clubs; working classes demanded more opportunities

A2 Socially exclusive clubs; few public facilities; not taught in state schools; expense of equipment and facilities

A3 Provided entertainment for the masses; commercial opportunities recognised by entrepreneurs; higher disposable income; more leisure time

A4 Model Course/military drill (1902) as a reaction to the Boer War; syllabuses of physical training

***examiner's* note** At this time, sport was becoming more organised, commercialised and defined by social class and was growing in importance nationally.

Interwar years (1918–39) I

Q1 The interwar years brought economic problems. What were they?

Q2 What was the effect of the First World War on women's lives?

Q3 Although opportunities in sport increased, why were there still fewer opportunities for the working classes?

Q4 The Women's League of Health and Beauty often put on mass gymnastic-style displays. Why was this considered acceptable for women?

ANSWERS

the period between the First World War and the Second World War

A1 General strike, 1926; depression, 1930s; high unemployment

A2 Women had contributed to the war effort; emerged more independent and confident; working-class women were still much more restricted than men and than middle-class women

A3 Public provision had slowed down; working classes could not afford membership of the more exclusive clubs; sport was still controlled by middle-class and upper-class amateurs

A4 Non-contact; non-competitive; demonstration of graceful movement; following instructions; not too strenuous; reflected understanding of growing need for health and fitness

***examiner's* note** A social-class divide in sport continued but there was steady growth in participation across all classes.

Interwar years (1918–39) II

Q1 What factors meant that greyhound racing became popular with the working classes?

Q2 Why did feats such as the Channel swim by Gertrude Ederle in 1926 cause so much public interest?

Q3 Why were British sports teams beginning to fail in international events during the interwar years?

Q4 Why did the state/government begin to influence recreation and sport in the interwar years?

ANSWERS

A1 Adaptable to urban environments; use of football pitches; purpose-built stadiums could be constructed quickly and cheaply; meetings held in evenings, after work (often five times a week); working classes were targets for commercialised sport; opportunity to make money easily

A2 Media coverage; swimming was part of physical education in schools; interest in rare female achievements; interest in human potential

A3 Other countries started catching up; lack of facilities and funding; talent drawn from a narrow social base; amateur approach still dominant

A4 To improve health and control leisure time of the masses

***examiner's* note** The relative influences of wealth, leisure time and social status are similar for many activities.

1939–45 and postwar Britain

Q1 What was the effect of the Second World War on physical education in schools?

Q2 What characterised sport in the second half of the twentieth century?

Q3 The C.................. C.................. of P.................. R..................
was established in 1935.

Q4 What led to Lord's abandoning the traditional cricket fixture 'gentlemen versus players' in 1962, resulting in all participants being called 'cricketers'?

ANSWERS

Britain during and after the Second World War

A1 Destruction of facilities and consequent extensive rebuilding; therapeutic effect of exercise recognised; use of obstacle training for soldiers led to introduction of apparatus in schools; more female teachers (as men enlisted)

A2 Sport became international; highly commercialised and accessible to most social groups

A3 Central Council of Physical Recreation

A4 The 'gentlemen' were having to work; it became more difficult to raise a team to play the 'players' or professionals

***examiner's* note** Professionalism began to dominate the sport scene in postwar Britain.

Government intervention

Q1 Why did British governments become involved in recreation, sport and physical education in the early twentieth century?

Q2 (a) What does 'centralised' mean?
(b) Give two examples of a centralised approach to PE.

Q3 Which physical activities did the Baths and Washhouses Act 1846 help to promote?

Q4 What was the significance of physical education being under the control of the medical department of the Board of Education?

ANSWERS

the involvement of central government, for example in legislating on sport

A1 Health of the population; discipline and obedience of the working classes — form of social control; civilising of society

A2 (a) 'Drawn under central control', for example government directing policy across the country

(b) Choose from: Model Course 1902–04; syllabuses of physical training, 1904–33; National Curriculum, from 1988

A3 Swimming; diving; water polo

A4 Greater consideration given to the physical welfare of children; initial focus of teaching physical activities was on therapeutic and health-related rather than educational goals

***examiner's* note** The British government had little involvement in sport until the latter half of the twentieth century.

Influential characters

Q1 Dr T.................. A.................. was the headmaster of Rugby school from 1828 to 1842.

Q2 *T.................. B..................'s Schooldays*, by Thomas Hughes, reflected life at Rugby public school in the nineteenth century.

Q3 This well-known family-run chocolate company was the first in the UK to implement the half-day Saturday.

Q4 Charles Kingsley was the leader of a movement in the nineteenth century that recognised the idea of the healthy body and mind to serve God. What was the movement called?

ANSWERS

A1 Thomas Arnold

A2 *Tom Brown*

A3 Cadbury

A4 Muscular Christianity

***examiner's* note** Check your specification to find out which influential people you should know about. You should be aware of:
- their role
- their attitude towards sport or physical education
- the influence they had on sport or physical education
- their reasons for promoting/discouraging sport or physical education

Amateurism I

Q1 Which social group devised the concept of amateurism in the nineteenth century?

Q2 Why did amateurism suit the upper classes?

Q3 What was meant by a 'gentleman amateur'?

Q4 In which sport were the Corinthian Casuals famous?

ANSWERS

the ideal that participation in sport should be for the love of it and not for monetary gain

A1 Upper classes

A2 They could afford to participate in sport for the love of it as they had enough money and leisure time

A3 Someone drawn from the upper classes; received no payment for his participation in sport

A4 Association football

***examiner's* note** Sports have undergone major changes in their amateur/professional status. These codes are determined socially and are therefore subject to change. It is important that you use certain sports to highlight issues in your answers. Cricket, rugby and rowing are useful examples in this case.

Amateurism II

Q1 What is a 'shamateur'?

Q2 National governing bodies set up t.................. f.................. to hold money for athletes until they retired from sport.

Q3 In what way has the ideal of amateurism restricted the development of some sports in the modern-day era?

Q4 'Fair play' is the bedrock of amateurism. What type of behaviour is covered by this term?

ANSWERS

the ideal that participation in sport should be for the love of it and not for monetary gain

A1 An amateur who receives 'under-the-table' payments

A2 Trust funds

A3 Amateur sports have treated money as an unnecessary factor, which has led to an inability to attract funding and has restricted the growth of the sports

A4 Playing according to the rules; the idea of friendship and respect for others; a display of sportsmanship

***examiner's* note** The social class with which a sport was originally identified was likely to determine whether it was amateur or professional. For example, lawn tennis was adopted by the middle classes and therefore remained an amateur sport until well into the twentieth century.

Amateurism III

Q1 In which sport was there a manual labour clause that excluded the working classes from participating?

Q2 'Gentlemen versus players' was a fixture in which sport?

Q3 In which sport was there a breakaway movement in 1894–95, leading to a north/south divide in terms of the amateur/professional status of the game?

Q4 Why did the gentleman amateur not mind competing against the working-class professional?

ANSWERS

the ideal that participation in sport should be for the love of it and not for monetary gain

A1 Rowing

A2 Cricket

A3 Rugby football

A4 There was no shame if the gentleman amateur lost because he was not being paid; he did not train as seriously as the professional

***examiner's* note** The amateur code was devised by the upper classes in nineteenth-century England. Amateurism had a financial distinction as well as a social-class distinction.

Professionalism

Q1 Why did professional football become so popular in the nineteenth century?

Q2 The gladiator in ancient Rome was the first professional sportsman. What similarities are there between a gladiator and a professional footballer today?

Q3 What characterised the professional sportsman in nineteenth-century England?

Q4 What were 'broken-time payments'?

ANSWERS

the pursuit of a sporting activity for financial gain or as a means of earning livelihood

A1 Offered a way out of factory work; local heroes; workers could afford gate entry fees; entertainment for half-day Saturday; railways allowed transport of spectators; accepted by schools and churches

A2 Injury can end career; livelihood earned from the sport; entertaining spectators; 'owned' by an employer; bought and sold as a commodity

A3 Working-class; trained seriously; specialised; earned money from sport

A4 Payments made to compensate working-class players for loss of earnings while playing sports

***examiner's* note** The concepts of professionalism and amateurism continue to change. Some specifications may require you to chart these changes from the nineteenth century onwards; others may deal with the terms' origins.

Professional sport

Q1 At which sport was a 'professional waterman' proficient?

Q2 Pedestrianism was one of the earliest professional sports in England. How would you describe this sport?

Q3 In cricket, 'gentlemen versus players' was very popular. Explain what this meant.

Q4 Why did the professional game of rugby league develop in the north of England?

ANSWERS

sport organised for financial gain

A1 Rowing

A2 An early form of race-walking that attracted thousands of spectators

A3 'Gentlemen' were the upper-class amateurs and 'players' were the working-class professionals

A4 The north was the industrial heartland of England; working-class people who wanted to play the game had to be able to earn money from their sport because they had no other source of livelihood, unlike their upper-class counterparts

examiner's note Professional sport became linked with the idea that winning is the most important thing; the upper classes in British society felt that this way ethical and moral values were undermined. In Britain, professionalism became associated with the working classes and was treated in a derogatory manner by the higher social classes.

Social reforms

Q1 What were the effects of the Factory Acts and Sir John Lubbock's Act in the nineteenth century?

Q2 What word beginning with 'p' describes people who carry out benevolent or charitable acts?

Q3 What was the temperance movement?

Q4 What did the Suffragettes fight for?

ANSWERS

changes to working and living conditions of the poor, leading to improvements in morals, behaviour and provision of recreation facilities

A1 Reduced working hours, and therefore increased leisure time, for the working classes

A2 Philanthropists

A3 A movement to draw the working classes away from pubs and alcohol

A4 Universal suffrage, i.e. votes for women as well as men; more broadly, female liberation and equal rights for women

examiner's note Any change in society will be reflected in or have a legacy for sport and recreation.

British Empire

Q1 Which queen ruled during the golden age of the British Empire?

Q2 What well-known saying, involving the sun, refers to the wide extent of the former British Empire?

Q3 Which sports were imported into Britain from colonised countries?

Q4 Where and when was the Boer War fought?

ANSWERS

the colonisation of many countries by Great Britain, which led to the export of its cultural activities, such as sports

A1 Queen Victoria

A2 'The sun never sets on the British Empire'

A3 Polo; badminton; lacrosse

A4 In South Africa, from 1899 to 1902

***examiner's* note** Considering the influence of the British Empire will help you to understand the impact that Britain had on the rest of the world, especially the export of its modern forms of sport.

Olympism

Q1 Which British institutions inspired Baron Pierre de Coubertin to re-establish the modern Olympic Games?

Q2 State two goals of the Olympic movement.

Q3 Finish the Olympic oath: 'In the name of all the competitors I promise that we shall take part in these Olympic Games respecting and abiding by the rules which govern them, committing ourselves to a sport without doping and without drugs,...'

Q4 Which nineteenth-century British sport concepts are similar to Olympism?

ANSWERS

a concept balancing the mind and body which encourages effort, educational values and ethical behaviour

A1 Nineteenth-century English public schools

A2 Choose from: personal excellence; sport as education; cultural exchange; mass participation; fair play; international understanding

A3 …'in the true spirit of sportsmanship, for the glory of sport and the honour of our teams'

A4 Athleticism; amateurism

***examiner's* note** Be prepared to discuss whether the values of Olympism are still relevant today.

Public school I

Q1 What were the characteristics of nineteenth-century English public schools?

Q2 How did the technical development of games occur in public schools?

Q3 How did public schools influence the spread of sports into wider society?

Q4 Name three of the original English public schools.

ANSWERS

a private, independent, fee-paying school

A1 For the upper classes; exclusive; fee-paying; single-sex; non-local; residential; strict discipline

A2 Formal rules developed; competitive structure via house system; codification led to inter-school fixtures; skills and strategies developed; concept of captain's 'Blues' developed; facilities and equipment

A3 Old boys' networks; positions of leadership, e.g. clergy to parishioners, officers to troops, officials across British Empire; development of clubs; schools provided facilities

A4 Choose from: Eton; Harrow; Rugby; Shrewsbury; Charterhouse; Westminster; Winchester; St Paul's; Merchant Taylors'

***examiner's* note** The public schools were for the sons and (later) daughters of the gentry, who would become leaders in their society. Team games were considered suitable for building character, such as bravery, loyalty and morality.

Public school II

Q1 What was the influential outcome of the Clarendon Commission in 1864?

Q2 Why were team games so highly valued by public schools?

Q3 What did self-government mean in terms of the organisation of team games in public schools?

Q4 Suggest three reasons why cricket acted as a form of social control for boys in public schools.

ANSWERS

a private, independent, fee-paying school

A1 It produced a government report that recognised for the first time the educational value of team games

A2 Character training; English origin; recreational value; moral values of teamwork and sportsmanship; physical health; athleticism; leadership

A3 The pupils were in charge of organising the activities themselves

A4 Choose from: rules meant a code of behaviour; younger boys helped the older boys in practice; junior teachers acted as players and coaches; headmaster gained respect of boys by encouraging the game; respect for role of captain; boys who didn't play could watch and support; could take place within school grounds

***examiner's* note** Team games indigenous to the UK had high status and were acceptable to parents.

Girls' public school

Q1 Why was athleticism delayed in girls' public schools?

Q2 Why did sports such as tennis and hockey become appropriate for middle-class girls in public schools?

Q3 How did public schools help in the emancipation of women?

Q4 Which influential woman established one of the first physical education teacher-training colleges, at Dartford? What was her role in the development of physical activities in state schools?

ANSWERS

a private, independent, fee-paying school for upper- and middle-class girls

A1 Medical opinion was against women participating in strenuous physical activity; considered inappropriate for women to be competitive

A2 Acceptable to parents as already established as club sports in society

A3 Gave an intellectual education; encouraged girls to question their role in society; physical activities gave them a competitive edge

A4 Martina Bergman-Österberg; she became Lady Superintendent of the London School Board and encouraged the use of Swedish Gymnastics as a suitable activity for the working classes

***examiner's* note** Schools for girls were modelled on those for boys, but women had to fight for the right to have competitive physical activities. Their success reflected changing social attitudes towards women.

Proprietary college

Q1 Why did the middle classes have to establish their own public schools?

Q2 What derogatory term did the gentry use for the new middle-class schools, which were copies of the elite schools?

Q3 What does 'Philistine' mean in relation to the new middle-class schools?

Q4 What prevented the middle classes from sending their children to the prestigious public schools when they could afford to?

ANSWERS

a nineteenth-century, middle-class, private, independent, fee-paying school

A1 Although they could afford to send their children to the established schools, they were still not accepted as social equals by the gentry

A2 'Philistine schools'

A3 Lacking in culture and tradition

A4 Although they had amassed the money, they were seen as lacking the necessary culture and breeding

***examiner's* note** The proprietary colleges or Philistine schools were for the sons and daughters of the middle classes who were not able to attend the established, prestigious schools controlled by the gentry. The proprietary colleges provided a reputable education for leadership roles in society, particularly among the professions (e.g. law, medicine).

Athleticism

Q1 How does 'athleticism' differ from modern-day 'fitness'?

Q2 What is implied by the words 'physical' and 'moral' with reference to the phrase 'physical endeavour with moral integrity'?

Q3 How did the cult of athleticism help the boys from public schools to become leaders in society?

Q4 How did games match the concept of athleticism?

ANSWERS

physical endeavour with moral integrity

A1 Fitness does not incorporate any moral qualities

A2 Physical: health; break from study; energetic; competitive. Moral: teamwork; catharsis; channelling of energies; leadership

A3 Organisational experience; social contacts through sport; competition in sport reflected capitalist society; captains in sport = captains of industry; healthy lifestyle gave them an advantage over the working classes; teamwork fostered effective working practices

A4 Games involved teams; boys worked together; developed comradeship, loyalty and self-sacrifice; conformity to a code of ethics; physical struggle in a common cause

***examiner's* note** Athleticism began to dominate public school life as the prestige gained from winning in sport fixtures became increasingly important.

University

Q1 What effect did universities have on the development of sport in the nineteenth century?

Q2 What does 'melting-pot' refer to in connection with universities and the development of games?

Q3 What does 'codification' mean?

Q4 What is meant by a 'blue'?

ANSWERS

A1 Codified rules; raised sporting standards; developed a variety of activities; technical development of activities; established 'colours' to recognise sporting prowess; spread the code of athleticism across society

A2 Individual schools' rules were first thrown together, then codified or universalised

A3 The systematic organisation of methods, rules and procedures into one recognised system

A4 An award conferred on Oxford and Cambridge university students for sporting prowess

***examiner's* note** The universities played a part in the codification of sport and its spread through society.

Governing body

Q1 Why were governing bodies initially established?

Q2 What was the role of a governing body in the nineteenth century?

Q3 Why were the majority of governing bodies amateur in their administration?

Q4 Why did many governing bodies prevent professionals from competing in their sport?

ANSWERS

an organisation responsible for the administration of a particular sport

A1 Sports were becoming popular — rules needed to be agreed nationally, enabling clubs and individuals to compete on equal terms

A2 To establish codified rules; to administer the sport locally and nationally

A3 Governing bodies were established by the 'old boys' of the public schools, who adopted the amateur ethos of sport

A4 They did not believe in material rewards for participating in sport; amateurs did not train seriously in the way that the professionals did; amateurs did not want to compete against, or be beaten by, their social inferiors

***examiner's* note** The values of the social class that controlled a particular governing body would be influential for centuries to come. As sport became institutionalised, more barriers were created to limit the opportunities for the lower classes.

State school

Q1 Why was Forster's Education Act of 1870 a watershed for state education?

Q2 Name three characteristics of the early state schools.

Q3 Why was there a delay in the provision of team games in state schools?

Q4 What was the role of the working classes at the end of the nineteenth century?

ANSWERS

a school maintained by public spending

A1 It marked the beginning of compulsory state education for all children

A2 Choose from: catered for working-class children; local; free; poor conditions; mixed sexes

A3 Lack of facilities; working classes not considered to have a right to recreation; working classes deemed not to need character development

A4 To be employees; to be troops; to accept their place in society without question; to obey the ruling class

***examiner's* note** State education catered for the working classes, who would become the followers in society — those who took orders and knew their place. The physical activities offered had to be appropriate for schools with limited facilities. It was thought that the working classes had no need for recreational activities, as they would grow up to work long hours.

Swedish Gymnastics

Q1 Give three reasons why Swedish Gymnastics was considered suitable for state schools.

Q2 Who was called 'the father of gymnastics'?

Q3 Why was gymnastics not so popular in public schools?

Q4 Why did the Model Course replace Swedish Gymnastics?

ANSWERS

a military drill style of gymnastics

A1 Choose from: promoted fitness of working classes; command/obey style suited to instilling discipline among working classes; catered for large numbers in a small space; cost-effective; free standing — no apparatus required

A2 Per Henrik Ling

A3 Foreign influence; individual rather than a team activity; not considered to have a moral influence on the pupils

A4 Following defeat in the Boer War, Swedish gymnastics was considered ineffective in developing the fitness of the working classes for war

***examiner's* note** Swedish Gymnastics was adopted by the Board of Education as a form of physical exercise because it was seen as helping to prepare working-class children for the workplace and war. It was similar to military drill in that it required no equipment and was based on an instructional style.

Model Course

Q1 What problems did the heavy losses in the Boer War highlight for the British government?

Q2 What was the effect of the Boer War (1899–1902) on activities in state schools?

Q3 What were three main aims of the Model Course with reference to the working classes?

Q4 Give three characteristics of military drill.

ANSWERS

a drill regime used in state schools from 1902 to 1904

A1 Lack of fitness and discipline of the troops

A2 It led to the introduction of the Model Course

A3 Increase fitness; improve familiarity with weapons and combat; improve discipline and obedience

A4 Choose from: command/obey; commands issued by non-commissioned officer; regimented lines; class response — all doing the same actions

***examiner's* note** Military drill was adopted as a form of physical exercise in state schools because it helped to prepare the working classes in fitness and obedience for the workplace and war.

Syllabuses of physical training

Q1 Why was there a need for syllabuses of physical training?

Q2 Outline the nature of the early syllabuses (1904–09).

Q3 What does 'centralised' mean in relation to the syllabuses of physical training?

Q4 Give three main ways in which the 1933 syllabus differed from the 1919 syllabus.

ANSWERS

guidelines for state school exercise courses from 1904 to 1933

A1 Model Course considered unsuitable for children; no specialist PE teachers; fitness and health of working classes still a priority; government wanted control over state schools

A2 Still instructional; emphasis on therapeutic effect; mainly exercises in unison; taken by the teacher; little variety of activity; no equipment

A3 The syllabuses, which all state schools had to follow, were decided by the central government

A4 1933 syllabus: lessons less centralised; individual response rather than group response; element of small playground games rather than major team games; fun and enjoyment more important than previously

***examiner's* note** Questions on this topic will often require you to compare an earlier and later syllabus.

Movement approach

Q1 If ‘movement’ was the key term in the 1950s, what was the key term in the nineteenth-century state schools?

Q2 What was the role of the teacher in the movement approach?

Q3 What skills were encouraged in the movement approach?

Q4 Name two activities that epitomised the movement approach in the 1950s.

ANSWERS

the encouragement of freedom, self-discovery and self-expression in physical education

A1 Drill

A2 Helping to learn; guiding in discovery or investigation

A3 Expressiveness/creativity; individual response to tasks; decision-making; dance; gymnastics; body management skills

A4 Modern educational dance; modern educational gymnastics

***examiner's* note** In state schools, the movement approach rivalled team games due to the perceived educational benefits. Public schools maintained their passion for team games and sports.

Moving and Growing

Q1 What two major influences were incorporated within the *Moving and Growing* programme?

Q2 What does 'child-centred' mean?

Q3 What does 'decentralised' mean in relation to the *Moving and Growing* programme?

Q4 What was the name of the other programme developed by the Ministry of Education to complement *Moving and Growing*?

ANSWERS

a 1952 Ministry of Education publication for use in primary schools

A1 Obstacle training from the army; movement training from the centres of dance, such as Laban

A2 Catering for the development of children's needs, particularly physical, intellectual, social and emotional

A3 Teachers had more choice over what was taught, compared with the earlier syllabuses of physical training; the teaching style was heuristic rather than instructional; the teacher developed individual responses rather than class responses

A4 *Planning the Programme*

examiner's note *Moving and Growing* and *Planning the Programme* emphasised the radical change in philosophy regarding physical education and the working classes. They encouraged the use of creativity, decision-making and problem-solving.

Teaching style

Q1 Give three ways in which the content of a PE lesson in 1953 would differ from that of a physical training class in 1906.

Q2 Give three lesson objectives of a PE lesson in 1953.

Q3 Give three ways in which the role of the teacher would differ in a PE lesson in 1953 compared to a physical training class in 1906.

Q4 What does 'heuristic' mean?

ANSWERS

A1 Choose from: in 1953 — less regimented; activities child-centred rather than adult-based; skills/dance/educational gymnastics instead of drill movement; more energetic; use of apparatus

A2 Choose from: development of movement skills/educational gymnastics/dance; fun; encourage expression and decision-making skills

A3 Choose from: in 1953 — teacher planned own work; concerned with child development; interaction with children; individual response sought; in 1906 — instructional style; syllabus followed closely; maintain order and discipline; whole-class response required

A4 'Encouraging learning by discovery'

***examiner's* note** You will need to compare approaches from military drill, syllabuses of physical training, *Moving and Growing* and the present-day National Curriculum.

Blood sport

Q1 What are the historical characteristics of blood sports?

Q2 Why did many blood sports decline and/or disappear?

Q3 What was a bear garden?

Q4 Why was cockfighting so popular?

ANSWERS

a leisure activity involving the killing of animals

A1 Violent; gambling involved; enjoyment in infliction of pain; available in rural and urban areas; enjoyed by all social groups but particularly the working and upper classes

A2 Acts of Parliament banned them; moral outlook of the middle classes resulted in the civilising of society; urbanisation stimulated new concepts of recreation

A3 An area in a town where bears were kept to be baited by dogs

A4 Opportunity for gambling; easily accessible and simple to stage; limited facilities needed; fair/close fights between well-matched cocks

***examiner's* note** Blood sports were a feature of a violent and cruel society. The emergence of the middle classes with their civilising and moral impact led to many of these activities being banned. The debate about foxhunting continues today at the highest levels.

Swimming

Q1 Why were spa towns such as Bath popular?

Q2 Why did swimming become popular in the eighteenth and nineteenth centuries?

Q3 How did industrialisation lead to a decline in swimming as a popular recreation?

Q4 What was the purpose of the Baths and Washhouses Act 1840?

ANSWERS

propelling oneself through the water using only the arms and legs

A1 Spas were considered to have a therapeutic and medical value; fashionable society gathered at spa towns for social occasions; escape from growing industrial towns

A2 Development of facilities, clubs and new techniques; heroic figures, such as Captain Webb, who swam the Channel; health and hygiene with the Baths and Washhouses Act; included in the Olympics; everyone could participate; development of Amateur Swimming Association

A3 Resulted in polluted rivers and the heavy use of waterways as transport routes; privatisation of property on waterfronts restricted access

A4 To promote health and hygiene among the industrial working classes

***examiner's* note** Swimming became a rational form of recreation as rules and facilities were developed.

Racket sport

Q1 Why was real tennis an activity enjoyed by the upper classes?

Q2 Why was rackets suitable for the lower social classes?

Q3 Which modern game is derived from the traditional game of rackets?

Q4 Why was lawn tennis adopted by the middle classes?

ANSWERS

a sport that uses a racket to hit an object (usually a ball)

A1 One of the earliest rational sports; sophisticated game with complex, written rules; required expensive, indoor facilities; developed etiquette peculiar to the sport; individual game with spectator appeal

A2 It could take place wherever there was a wall; equipment could be hired from publicans; simpler game than real tennis

A3 Squash

A4 Affordable; could be played in large suburban gardens and private clubs; social activity for both sexes; rational, rule-based and civilised activity; set middle classes apart from the lower classes

examiner's note The level of sophistication of a racket sport reflected the participants' wealth.

Team games

Q1 What changes to mob football turned it into a rational activity?

Q2 How did rugby football match the concept of athleticism?

Q3 What is meant by the term 'games cult' in relation to nineteenth-century public schools?

Q4 Why did rugby split into the northern and southern codes in 1895?

ANSWERS

games or sports involving groups of people working together to achieve a common goal

A1 Played regularly; codified rules; regional and national development; highly structured, with a set number of players and boundaries; division of labour; skill rather than force

A2 Physically energetic; required teamwork; team more important than the individual; rule-based/rational activity; took place on the school grounds; developed leadership and response to leadership

A3 Team games were given a high status in public schools; much time was given to practise and improve standards of play; in some schools, team games became more prominent than academic excellence; a devotion to games

A4 Northern clubs wanted to make 'broken-time' payments; southern clubs wanted a strict maintenance of amateurism

***examiner's* note** Team games became popular mostly because they had the approval of public schools. They were bound by rules and etiquette, teamwork and loyalty.

Outdoor activity

Q1 What was the significance of the term ‘escape’ in relation to outdoor or adventurous activities?

Q2 What was the significance of the Romantic movement for outdoor recreation activities?

Q3 Give three reasons why rock climbing became popular in the nineteenth century.

Q4 What was the influence of the railways on outdoor activities?

ANSWERS

a physical, challenging activity that takes place in the natural environment

A1 Industrialisation led to people needing to escape from the polluted cities

A2 Poems by the Romantic poets such as Wordsworth attracted the middle and, later, the working classes to visit areas such as the Lake District, where rambling, cycling and rock climbing became popular

A3 Choose from: linked to the Romantic movement; upper classes went to the Alps; interest in the natural world; working classes gained access via the railways; increased interest in health; locations close to large centres of population; escape towns/ cities; seeking adventure

A4 Cheap and easy access to the countryside; could take a bicycle on the train and purchase a rover ticket; rambling and fishing became popular

examiner's note Outdoor activities often involve dangerous and challenging situations, and possibly the overcoming of natural obstacles or terrain.

Individual activity I

Q1 Why was cycling a suitable activity for the middle classes?

Q2 P.................. was an early form of race walking.

Q3 Why did athletics become popular in the nineteenth century?

Q4 What factors caused the game of golf to change from a pastime for all social classes to a more exclusive game?

ANSWERS

a sport in which one person performs alone to achieve his/her aim

A1 Alternative to the horse (used by upper classes); suitable for urban environments; product of the Industrial Revolution (supported by the middle classes); popular with middle-class women seeking more freedom; working classes could not afford it; development of clubs

A2 Pedestrianism

A3 Encouraged in public schools; competitive; revival of Olympic Games; could be participated in at amateur and professional level

A4 Enclosure of land; development of exclusive clubs; developments in equipment priced out the lower classes; administration of the game was in the hands of the middle and upper classes

examiner's note Traditionally, individual activities had a lower status in the UK than team games as they were not considered to have character-building qualities.

Individual activity II

Q1 H.............. and h.............., developed in nineteenth-century public schools, was the forerunner of what we know today as cross-country.

Q2 Why was rowing popular in the nineteenth century?

Q3 How did athletics reflect the spirit of athleticism in public schools?

Q4 Why was there a delay in the introduction of athletics for women?

ANSWERS

a sport in which one person performs alone to achieve his/her aim

A1 Hare; hounds

A2 Long history as a functional and recreational activity; all social classes could participate (e.g. working-class 'watermen' and public schools; races and regattas combined competition and social occasions; media coverage

A3 Physically vigorous activity; respectable, highly organised; codes of behaviour, e.g. sportsmanship; encouraged teamwork and loyalty to a house; annual sports day was a display for governors and parents

A4 Rational, amateur athletics started by men; middle-class women were not encouraged to participate in sport in public; women should be genteel and not sweat; not taught in girls' public schools; disapproved of by medical profession

examiner's note Many of the details about public schools, amateurism and professionalism can be examined through various physical activities, including athletics.

Play

Q1 Why is play said to be spontaneous?

Q2 What motivates children to play?

Q3 What is meant by 'role rehearsal'? Give an example of a children's play activity that reflects this.

Q4 Apart from enjoyment, what motivates adults to play?

ANSWERS

a voluntary, spontaneous activity, carried out at leisure and for fun

A1 There are no predetermined or set rules to adhere to, e.g. no fixed time, boundaries or number of players

A2 Intrinsic motivation, to have fun

A3 Children master reality through play that mimics real life, e.g. 'mummies and daddies'

A4 Escape from reality; catharsis; release from stress

***examiner's* note** In terms of organisation, the concept of play is at the other end of the spectrum from sport. Therefore, if you reverse many answers about play, you will correctly answer equivalent questions on sport. For example, sport is highly structured, with set, externally enforced rules, fixed boundaries and a pre-determined number of players.

Physical recreation

Q1 Physical recreation is also known as a.................. l.................. .

Q2 State three characteristics of physical recreation.

Q3 Give two benefits of physical recreation for society.

Q4 What organisations are the main providers of physical recreation in a local community?

ANSWERS

a physical activity carried out voluntarily within leisure time

A1 Active leisure

A2 Choose from: modified rules; casual attitude; non-serious outcomes; no obligation

A3 Choose from: social control; integration of communities; people develop skills; health of a population; economic profit

A4 Local authorities; voluntary-sector sports clubs; private clubs

***examiner's* note** Leisure is the time; recreation is the activity. In terms of how organised it is, recreation falls between play and sport.

Leisure

Q1 What are the three main prerequisites of leisure?

Q2 How can work affect leisure?

Q3 How can leisure provision aid social control?

Q4 State two benefits of leisure for an individual.

ANSWERS

a time for activities to which an individual can turn at will

A1 Free time; opportunity; choice

A2 It determines the amount of free time and energy left for leisure

A3 It gives the population a variety of activities that are socially acceptable; avoids boredom; reduces crime rates

A4 Choose from: relief of stress; improved physical and mental health; self-fulfilment

***examiner's* note** Leisure opportunities have depended largely on which social group an individual belongs to. The working classes in the industrialised world have had fewer opportunities than the middle and upper classes. Women have traditionally had fewer opportunities than men.

Physical education

Q1 Give three main aims of physical education.

Q2 How many Key Stages are there in the National Curriculum?

Q3 What roles, other than purely as a performer, does the National Curriculum require pupils to perform?

Q4 What are the advantages of having a National Curriculum for physical education?

ANSWERS

the inculcation of skills and values through physical activity in an educational setting

A1 Choose from: development of motor skills; development of flexibility, stamina and strength; appreciation of a range of activities and positive values; development of self-esteem; understanding the need for a healthy lifestyle

A2 Four

A3 Critical performer; coach (analysing strengths and weaknesses); officiator; leader (e.g. captain); choreographer; informed spectator

A4 It provides uniformity of experience; sets standards and targets; makes teachers accountable; puts physical education on a par with other subjects

***examiner's* note** Physical education is a concept that has developed to give the teaching of physical activities or sports an educational focus, compared with the more one-dimensional concept of 'physical training', which considers only body development.

Outdoor and adventurous activity

Q1 What types of activity are included in these terms?

Q2 What is the difference between outdoor education and outdoor recreation?

Q3 What is meant by (a) objective danger and (b) subjective danger?

Q4 Why have outdoor and adventurous activities become so popular?

ANSWERS

a physical, challenging activity that takes place in the natural environment

A1 Examples include rock climbing, skiing, canoeing, paragliding and sailing

A2 Outdoor education refers to activities organised in an educational setting (e.g school ski trip); outdoor recreation refers to activities carried out in an individual's free time (e.g. ski holiday with friends)

A3 (a) Danger from the environment — the individual has little control over it

(b) Danger under the control of the individual

A4 Escape from urban life; appreciation of the natural environment; increasing opportunities; fashion for extreme sports; media coverage; youth culture; role models

***examiner's* notes** Do not use the terms 'fresh air' or 'outdoors' — use 'natural environment'. Consider what these activities offer that other sports may not.

Extra-curricular sport

Q1 Compare extra-curricular sport and physical education.

Q2 How have recent governments tried to improve the links between schools and sports clubs in the community?

Q3 Give two advantages of improving links between schools and local sports clubs.

Q4 Give two disadvantages of encouraging schools to become the 'nurseries of sporting talent'.

ANSWERS

opportunities provided for children to participate in school sport outside the normal school timetable

A1 School sport is voluntary and focuses on improving performance levels; physical education is compulsory and focuses on the needs and education of the child

A2 Sports college status; National Junior Sports Programme; Sportsmark/Activemark; school sport coordinators; PE and School Sport and Club Link Strategy (PESSCL)

A3 Continued participation on leaving school; improvement of standards

A4 Choose from: aims of physical education are different from those of sport; the teacher is not necessarily a specialist coach; most children cannot become top performers

***examiner's* note** You will be required to discuss whether or not physical education and school sport should be more closely related.

Sport

Q1 What does the term 'institutionalised' mean when referring to sport?

Q2 Give three characteristics of sport.

Q3 Suggest three benefits to the individual when participating in sport.

Q4 Suggest three ways in which society may benefit from success in sport at elite level.

ANSWERS

competitive activity involving physical exertion or relatively complex physical skills

A1 Set rules enforced by officials, clubs and governing bodies; rationalised activities involving strategies and tactics; formally learnt skills

A2 Choose from: fixed time and boundaries; set numbers of players; fixed rules; advanced skills; serious outcomes; extrinsic rewards

A3 Choose from: self-satisfaction; challenge; emotional release; development of physical skills; socialisation; health and fitness

A4 Choose from: development of role models; encouragement of participation at grass-roots level; social integration; economic profit; national prestige; national 'feel-good factor'

***examiner's* note** In terms of organisation, the concept of sport is at the other end of the spectrum from play.

Participation pyramid

Q1 What does 'foundation' refer to in relation to the participation pyramid?

Q2 How does the participation level differ from the foundation level on the participation pyramid?

Q3 Of what standard might a performer be if he/she is at the performance level of sport?

Q4 What do 'excellence' and 'elite' refer to in relation to the participation pyramid?

ANSWERS

a scale of involvement in competition sport

A1 The introduction to basic sport skills, mostly via the physical education programme in schools

A2 The individual participates out of choice and extends an initial interest in an activity; this may be evidenced by participating in extra-curricular activities in schools or by joining a sports club

A3 High club or regional standard, committed to training and perfecting skills

A4 Excellence can be reached in terms of personal achievement; elite is the level that only a few achieve

***examiner's* note** You need to know the main terms — foundation, participation, performance and excellence — and also be able to match these with sports policies and provision within society.

Administration of sport I

Q1 What does 'DCMS' stand for and what is the organisation's role in relation to sport?

Q2 What is meant by 'decentralised administration'?

Q3 What is the role of UK Sport?

Q4 Which two organisations have overall responsibility for disability sport in the UK?

ANSWERS

A1 Department of Culture, Media and Sport; it is the government department for sport, providing funding and policies

A2 The dispersal of power away from the centre towards outlying regions; government is organised into smaller units such as local authorities, which interpret government guidelines so as to meet their regional requirements

A3 To develop elite sport; attract major international events to the UK; develop a nationwide policy for issues such as coaching and doping; represent the UK internationally

A4 Disability Sport England and the English Federation of Disability Sport

***examiner's* note** Questions on organisations tend to focus on their functions and policies, rather than on how they are structured.

Administration of sport II

Q1 The British Sports Trust delivers four sports leader awards. What are they?

Q2 What are the core elements of the Active Programme run by Sport England?

Q3 Identify two initiatives of SportsCoach UK.

Q4 What are the three key levels of the World Class Performance Pathway operated by UK Sport?

ANSWERS

A1 Junior Sports Leader Award; Community Sports Leader Award; Higher Sports Leader Award; Basic Expedition Leader Award

A2 Active Schools; Active Communities; Active Sports; World Class Programme

A3 Choose from: UK Coaching Framework; UK Coaching Certificate; runs Coachwise Ltd

A4 World Class Podium, World Class Development and World Class Talent

***examiner's* note** Find out which organisations your specification requires you to know about.

Administration of sport III

Q1 Give two features of the Sportsmark policy.

Q2 What occurs when a school is given sports college status?

Q3 What does 'PESSCL' stand for and what does the initiative aim to do?

Q4 What is the role of SportsCoach UK?

ANSWERS

A1 Rewards schools for best practice in sport and physical education; includes Activemark, Sportsmark and Sports Partnership Mark

A2 Allowed to specialise in sport; given considerable funding; remit to develop community sport; heads a schools network linked by a school sports coordinator; has to draw up a development plan

A3 Physical Education, School Sport and Club Links; the PESSCL strategy improves links between schools and clubs and provides high-quality PE and school sport

A4 Provides educational and advisory service for coaches; develops sports science courses; produces coaching literature; runs a network of national coaching centres; develops coaching qualifications

***examiner's* note** UK Government intervention in sport has increased in the last 20 years.

Administration of sport IV

Q1 What is the public sector in sport?

Q2 What is the voluntary sector in sport?

Q3 Give two key features of the private sector in relation to leisure provision.

Q4 State two aims of the government's Best Value policy.

ANSWERS

A1 Business operations run by the local authority; trades on set prices/charges according to a preset budget; may involve subsidies

A2 Business operations run by members; run on a trust/charity basis; trades on normal profit/loss/breakeven; financed by members' fees

A3 Privately owned; trading on profit/loss; managed by owners and employees; must survive in open market

A4 Choose from: modernise local authorities; measure, manage and improve performance; improve the cost and quality of local services

***examiner's* note** You need to understand why local authority-owned leisure facilities are increasingly being run by private companies.

Administration of sport V

Q1 Name the elements of the TOP programme.

Q2 Step Into Sports helps young .... and volunteers.

Q3 Explain the following initiatives: Active Schools; Active Communities; Active Sports.

Q4 What does 'TASS' stand for and what does the initiative do?

ANSWERS

A1 TOP Tots; TOP Play (4–9 years); TOP Sport (7–11 years); TOP Sportsability (all ages); TOP Club; TOP Link; TOP Resources

A2 leaders

A3 Active Schools forms the foundation level of sport; Active Communities is concerned with breaking down the barriers to participation; Active Sports links the participation level of sport to excellence

A4 Talented Athlete Scholarship Scheme; supports athletes' training while in education; organisations involved include EIS, Sport England and UK Sport; also operates under the World Class Performance Pathway

examiner's note Sports policies focus on increasing participation at the grass-roots level and/or improving standards at the elite level.

National sport institutes

Q1 Outline the role of the English Institute of Sport (EIS).

Q2 What are the characteristics of the EIS, the Welsh Institute of Sport and the Scottish Institute of Sport?

Q3 What are the advantages of a regional approach to academies of sport?

Q4 How might centres of excellence help increase participation at grass-roots level?

ANSWERS

A1 Provides a nationwide network of world-class support services; nine regional hub sites; fosters talents of UK elite athletes

A2 Top-class coaching, facilities and scientific support; talented sports performers; lifestyle coaching; technical support; sports medicine

A3 Easier access across the UK; different sports can be focused on

A4 Facilities can be used by community; medal winners can motivate people to participate

***examiner's* note** You need to understand the advantages and disadvantages of providing support for elite athletes.

National governing bodies

Q1 What are the common functions of a national governing body?

Q2 What is a Whole Sport Plan?

Q3 Name the NGB for the following sports in the UK: tennis and football.

Q4 What are some of the challenges facing national governing bodies?

ANSWERS

a national governing body is responsible for its own sport, overseeing competitions and ensuring that internationally agreed rules are followed

A1 Ensures that rules and regulations set by ISF are followed; has a Who Sport Plan from grass-roots to elite sport; organises competitions; selects national teams; develops coaching/leadership schemes; liaises with other organisations such as Sport England and local clubs

A2 It is a plan for a sport, from grass-roots to elite level; outlines its vision; necessary in order to access funding; must meet Sport Englan objectives of 'grow, sustain, excel'

A3 Tennis = Lawn Tennis Association (LTA); Football = Football Association (FA)

A4 Development of more, different sports means decreasing numbers of participants in each sport; need to bridge the gap between school sport and club sport; pressures on amateur sports from professional sports; need to secure funding from a variety of sources; compete wi countries with systematic programmes to develop elite performers; must meet government targets

examiner's note Try to make sure you are familiar with the governing body for a variety of sports and research some of these bodies' policies.

Funding

Q1 Give two characteristics of the organisation called SportsAid.

Q2 Give three reasons to justify spending National Lottery money on sport.

Q3 How are amateur athletes funded in the UK?

Q4 How does the British Olympic Association fund its work to support Team GB?

ANSWERS

money set aside to support sport, which may be obtained from a variety of sources

A1 Raises its own funds from commercial, industrial and private sponsors; gives funds to top amateur junior and senior athletes

A2 Choose from: sport is a healthy pastime; releases government money for essential services; success leads to national pride; all sections of society benefit

A3 Sponsorship; lottery; grants; TASS; SportsAid; parents

A4 Raises its own funds from donations and commercial sponsorship

***examiner's* note** You do not need to know specific figures, but you do need to know how organisations raise money and how/why they spend it.

Culture I

Q1 The term s............... is used to describe how people learn the cultural norms and values of their society.

Q2 Sport in some societies originally had a functional or utilitarian purpose. Using an example, explain what this means.

Q3 Less economically developed countries often have a policy of selective sport. Using an example, explain what this means.

Q4 In what way do professional sports reflect a capitalist system?

ANSWERS

the way of life of a society, including its language, customs, dress, symbols and artefacts

A1 Socialisation

A2 Sporting activities were initially developed for survival, e.g. spear-throwing to hunt for food and for defence

A3 A country with limited resources will select a sport in which it is likely to achieve international success; e.g. Kenya and long-distance running

A4 Heavy emphasis on competition and winning; materialistic rewards; commercialism/sponsorship; individual effort and glory; business operations

***examiner's* note** Sports and physical activities reflect the culture of which they form a part. They should not be seen in isolation.

Culture II

Q1 The term d................ is used to describe behaviour that rejects the cultural norms and values of wider society.

Q2 What is 'high culture'?

Q3 Why is football an example of 'low culture'?

Q4 What is 'dominant culture'?

ANSWERS

the way of life of a society including its language, customs, dress, symbols and artefacts

A1 Deviance

A2 The type of pastimes or activities patronised by the elite in society; an example in sport may be polo because it is not easily accessible to the lower social classes

A3 It is easily accessible to lower social groups; it is based on immediate excitement and understanding

A4 The way of life of the group in society that controls the major social institutions such as the law, education and sport; in the UK this group would be white, male and middle class (the dominant cultural group does not necessarily have to be the majority, e.g. apartheid in South Africa)

***examiner's* note** 'Subculture' is a term used to describe a group that shares values and attitudes that are different from those of the dominant culture (e.g. hooligans, surfers).

Equal opportunities I

Q1 What is discrimination in terms of sport participation?

Q2 What is stereotyping and how does it affect participation in sport?

Q3 What is a target group, for Sport England?

Q4 Name three target groups identified by Sport England.

ANSWERS

providing everyone with the same chance to participate in recreational and sporting activities

A1 When opportunities to participate in activities are not available to all social groups

A2 A standardised image shared by members of a social group; it usually involves negative images of gender, disability or race, and can affect society's expectations of the sporting potential of certain social groups

A3 Any group identified by Sport England as needing special attention in order to raise participation levels

A4 Choose from: women; young people; ethnic-minority groups; people with disabilities; low socioeconomic groups

***examiner's* note** Different social groups that participate less in sporting activities face similar barriers, such as reduced access to facilities, resources and opportunities.

Equal opportunities II

Q1 What is upward social mobility in terms of successful sport participation?

Q2 How can positive sporting role models be influential in society?

Q3 What is inclusion in terms of sport participation?

Q4 What are the three main aims of Sport England?

ANSWERS

providing everyone with the same chance to participate in recreational and sporting activities

A1 Success in sport is often an avenue for upward social mobility because income can be generated and social status raised

A2 They influence young people in terms of aspirations and behaviour; they increase participation at the grass-roots level of a sport

A3 The needs, abilities and aspirations of everyone should be recognised, understood and met within a supportive environment; it is part of a government strategy to include social groups who suffer exclusion

A4 'Grow, sustain, excel'

***examiner's* note** 'Exclusion' is a label for what can happen when individuals or areas suffer a combination of linked problems, such as unemployment, low income, bad health or poor skills. It can have lasting effects in terms of recreation and socialising. Governments now regard sport and recreation as having wider benefits to society.

Equal opportunities for women I

Q1 What is sexism?

Q2 Suggest three barriers that women might face when participating in sport.

Q3 Suggest three strategies a sports club could introduce to attract more women to participate.

Q4 In what way is sport exempt from the Sex Discrimination Act?

ANSWERS

A1 The belief that one sex is inferior to the other

A2 Choose from: society's attitudes; lack of crèche facilities; less publicity and awareness of opportunities; fewer role models; fewer clubs and competitions

A3 Training and use of female coaches; increased publicity; improved facilities for mothers; female sections of clubs; female-specific competitions

A4 Competitive sport is excluded under Section 44 of the Act; separate competitions are allowed for men and women 'where physical strength, stamina or physique puts a woman at a disadvantage to the average man'

***examiner's* note** Questions can have either a historical or a contemporary focus.

Equal opportunities for women II

Q1 What stereotypical views discouraged women from participating in competitive sports from the early twentieth century?

Q2 What is the role of the Women's Sports Foundation in terms of participation in physical recreation and sport?

Q3 How could the media help to promote women in sport?

Q4 Why is aerobics considered a more suitable activity for women than weightlifting?

ANSWERS

issues that address the unequal role of women in sport

A1 Women were seen as: having a domestic role; being physically too weak; not having the psychological drive for competitive sport

A2 To provide opportunities; promote the benefits of participation; support associated organisations; raise awareness of the needs of women in sport; encourage women to play an active role in the development of their sport; publicise issues via *Women in Sport* magazine

A3 Raise the amount of coverage; help to attract sponsors; focus on grass-roots development as well as elite-level sport

A4 Developed for women; mostly female instructors; mostly non-competitive; physically tones the body rather than developing muscle

***examiner's* note** Things that can affect the participation of women in sport include society's attitudes and expectations, lower income, safety concerns and poor self-image.

Disability I

Q1 Outline the difference between integrated and segregated sport.

Q2 What is adapted sport?

Q3 What is the role of Disability Sport England (DSE) in relation to participation in physical recreation?

Q4 What does 'Paralympic' mean?

ANSWERS

a physical, sensory or mental impairment that adversely affects performance

A1 Integrated: able-bodied and disabled people take part together. Segregated: disabled people participate separately from the able-bodied

A2 A sport that has been modified to be appropriate for a particular type of disability, e.g. wheelchair basketball

A3 To provide opportunities; to promote the benefits of participation; to support associated organisations; to raise awareness of the abilities of disabled people; to encourage disabled people to play an active role in the development of their sport

A4 Run in parallel with the Olympic Games

***examiner's* note** You need to be able to discuss the advantages and disadvantages of participation in sport by people with disabilities.

Disability II

Q1 Suggest three barriers that disabled people might face when participating in a sport.

Q2 Suggest three strategies a sports club could introduce to attract more disabled people.

Q3 Give two advantages of integrated sport.

Q4 Give two advantages of segregated sport.

ANSWERS

a physical, sensory or mental impairment that adversely affects performance

A1 Choose from: society's attitudes; poor access to facilities; less publicity for opportunities; fewer role models, clubs and competitions

A2 Choose from: training and use of specialised coaches; increased publicity, improved access to facilities; having disabled sections of the club; specific competitions

A3 Choose from: allows integration of the community; raises self-esteem of disabled; maximises use of facilities

A4 Choose from: disabled can participate at their own pace; safer environment; success more likely

***examiner's* note** Social groups that are under-represented in sport participation will share similar problems, and so similar strategies to improve participation would be effective.

Ethnic minority group I

Q1 What is racism?

Q2 Suggest three barriers that ethnic minority groups might face in relation to participation in sport.

Q3 Suggest three strategies a sports club could introduce to attract more people from ethnic minority groups.

Q4 What is stacking in relation to ethnic minority groups in sport?

ANSWERS

a group that shares a common culture and forms a minority in a population

A1 The assumption that races have distinct characteristics determined by hereditary factors, endowing some races with intrinsic superiority

A2 Choose from: society's attitudes; stereotyping; less publicity and awareness of opportunities; fewer role models; discrimination; peer pressure; cultural and religious practices

A3 Choose from: reduce discrimination; increase publicity; employ ethnic minority coaches; challenge assumptions of stereotyping

A4 The disproportionate concentration of players from ethnic minorities in certain positions in a sports team, for example occupying outfield positions in baseball

***examiner's* note** Focus on issues specific to these groups. Try not to use general responses, such as 'fewer facilities' or 'less money'.

Ethnic minority group II

Q1 Why are there few coaches and managers from ethnic minority groups in the professional game of football in the UK?

Q2 How can any sport governing body attempt to reduce the effects of racism?

Q3 How can a person's religion affect their participation in sport?

Q4 How can physical education teachers influence sporting opportunities for children from ethnic minority groups?

ANSWERS

a group that shares a common culture and forms a minority in a population

A1 Discrimination — the selectors for managerial positions tend to be from white, middle-class backgrounds

A2 Initiate and support campaigns such as Kick It Out!; actively promote performers from ethnic minority groups; harsher punishments for offenders; equal opportunity employment policies; train coaches from ethnic minority groups

A3 Customs and dress codes; observance of holy days; possibly lower status given to sport

A4 Teacher's expectations/stereotypical beliefs can channel children into certain sports; effect can be positive or negative

***examiner's* note** Be prepared to show your understanding of the link between a specific sport and an ethnic group, for example cricket and Pakistanis.

Low socioeconomic group

Q1 What is exclusion?

Q2 Suggest three barriers that low socioeconomic groups face in relation to participation in sporting activities.

Q3 Suggest three strategies a sports club could introduce to attract more people from lower socioeconomic groups.

Q4 Why does the government's Strategy for Neighbourhood Renewal promote sport for disadvantaged/deprived areas?

ANSWERS

people of low income, poor social status and often limited educational experiences

A1 Isolation from society as a result of socioeconomic problems

A2 Society's attitudes; less awareness of opportunities and health issues; discrimination; cost of facilities; dominant middle-class values that operate in sports clubs/centres; poor health; low self-esteem

A3 Reduce discriminatory practices; subsidise costs; raise awareness of health issues; publicise opportunities; use positive role models

A4 Sport can make a valuable contribution to: lower long-term unemployment and crime; better health and qualifications; greater pride in individuals and their community

***examiner's* note** Many national governing bodies have specific policies to democratise their sport, for example the Lawn Tennis Association's inner-city tennis schemes.

Talent identification

Q1 Suggest two personal qualities a performer might possess that would help him or her achieve high standards of excellence.

Q2 Give three advantages of specialist sports schools.

Q3 Suggest two ways in which a governing body might improve the way in which it identifies talent.

Q4 What is meant by a systematic talent identification programme?

ANSWERS

the encouragement of young people to participate in the sport at which they are most likely to succeed

A1 Choose from physical or psychological qualities such as: fitness; skills; commitment; dedication

A2 Choose from: high-quality facilities; high-quality coaching; groups of talented young people together; competitive opportunities

A3 Choose from: develop talent identification programmes; widen base of participation; eliminate discrimination; improve quality of coaching at all levels; offer physical and psychological testing of young people

A4 A programme that has been developed methodically in an organised, coherent manner; often involves testing schoolchildren

***examiner's* note** Talent identification is a long-term development plan. It is costly and young talent does not always achieve its potential. You will need to provide arguments for and against such plans.

Elite sport I

Q1 How can a governing body support a young, talented performer?

Q2 How could a sports club be elitist?

Q3 What does 'UKSI' stand for, and what is the organisation's role?

Q4 What effects would be evident for a national governing body if the national team in its sport was to win a world championship?

ANSWERS

a category of sporting participation comprising the most talented people

A1 Talent identification programmes; provide effective coaching; structured competition; funding

A2 Limit access through cost of membership or according to ability levels, gender or age

A3 United Kingdom Sports Institute; a series of regional centres with the purpose of developing elite athletes

A4 Increased participation; increased funding; higher awareness/profile; more officials and coaches; development of all sections, e.g. women's/children's/disabled sport

***examiner's* note** You need to understand the link between increased participation at the grass-roots level and greater potential for the development of elite athletes.

Elite sport II

Q1 State three responsibilities of the British Olympic Association.

Q2 The British Olympic Association does not receive funding from central government. What is the advantage of this situation?

Q3 The Fédération Internationale de Football Association (FIFA) is an example of an international sports federation. Give two functions of such an organisation.

Q4 Give three disadvantages of focusing on elite sport.

ANSWERS

a category of sporting participation comprising the most talented people

A1 Encourage interest in the Olympic Games; organise and coordinate the British team; deal with public and press relations; raise its own funds; provide medical and careers advice for athletes

A2 The government cannot control how the BOA spends money or direct it not to attend an Olympic Games — it can only advise

A3 Choose from: organise events; arrange television and sponsorship contracts; formulate the rules for its sport

A4 It serves the interests of a minority; athletes can over-train, causing damage physically and psychologically; the 'win-at-all-costs' attitude can undermine the moral values of sport

***examiner's* note** You need to be aware of the specific policies covered by your specification.

Olympic Games I

Q1 The ancient Games were held every 4 years in honour of the God Z.......... .

Q2 Which Frenchman established the modern Olympic Games?

Q3 What is the motto of the Olympic Games?

Q4 What do the five rings represent?

ANSWERS

international multi-sport contest held every 4 years in a selected country

A1 Zeus

A2 Baron Pierre de Coubertin

A3 'Citius, altius, fortius', meaning 'swifter, higher, stronger'

A4 The five continents of Europe, Asia, Oceania, Africa and the Americas

***examiner's* note** The Olympic Games can be used to explore many aspects of the specification, for example the role of women, commercialism and doping.

Olympic Games II

Q1 Which organisation controls the Olympic Games?

Q2 What is the name of the national Olympic committee (NOC) in the UK?

Q3 Name one president of the International Olympic Committee since 1980.

Q4 Where does the majority of funding for the Olympic Games come from?

ANSWERS

international multi-sport contest held every 4 years in a selected country

A1 International Olympic Committee (IOC)

A2 British Olympic Association

A3 Juan Antonio Samaranch (1980–2001); Jacques Rogge (2001–present)

A4 Sales of television rights; sponsorship; merchandise licensing; ticket sales; coins and stamps

***examiner's* note** The Olympic movement raises the profile of many non-Olympic sports by incorporating them as demonstration events. Ultimately, these may be accepted as Olympic sports.

Olympic Games III

Q1 In which year and in which city did Hitler use the Olympic Games to promote the 'supremacy of the Aryan race'?

Q2 What tragedy occurred in Munich in 1972?

Q3 Why do cities submit bids in order to host the Games?

Q4 What does 'TOP' stand for in relation to Olympic marketing and what does it involve?

ANSWERS

international multi-sport contest held every 4 years in a selected country

A1 Berlin, 1936

A2 Israeli athletes and officials were assassinated by Palestinian guerillas

A3 Civic and national pride; political gain; economic benefits

A4 The Olympic Programme; allows exclusive rights to a few selected international companies

***examiner's* note** You need to be aware of which political incidents your specification requires you to know about.

Olympic Games IV

Q1 Give three key phrases to describe the Olympic ideal.

Q2 How do the ideals of the Olympic movement conflict with the ideals of professional sport?

Q3 Why do some governments fund Olympic and world-class performers?

Q4 In what way is the Olympic Games different from the World Cup?

ANSWERS

international multi-sport contest held every 4 years in a selected country

A1 Choose from: bringing nations together; taking part is more important than winning; respect for ethical and moral values; improving tolerance; respect for others; competing fairly

A2 Professional sport involves material rewards rather than participating for the love of sport; winning is more important than taking part

A3 Develop national pride; economic benefits; allow citizens to develop potential; promote political superiority; 'shop-window' effect; develop role-models

A4 The Games is a multi-sport event as opposed to a single-sport event

***examiner's* note** The modern commercial world of sport has threatened the amateur basis of the Games, yet this has helped to raise the Games's global profile.

Paralympic Games

Q1 Where did the Paralympic Games originate?

Q2 What is the symbol of the Games?

Q3 What is the difference between the Special Olympics and the Paralympics?

Q4 Which organisation runs the Paralympic Games?

ANSWERS

international multi-sport contest for the disabled, which runs parallel to the Olympic Games

A1 Stoke Mandeville Hospital

A2 The three 'Tae-Geuks', symbolising the human mind, body and spirit

A3 The Special Olympics serves mentally retarded youths and adults, while the Paralympics is for those with physical and sensory disabilities

A4 International Paralympic Committee

***examiner's* note** The Paralympic Games can be used to explore many aspects of the specification, such as the role of people with disabilities in society, the advantages of sport to people with disabilities and the status of elite disability sport compared with mainstream sport.

Football World Cup

Q1 Whose name is associated with the Cup itself?

Q2 How often is the World Cup held?

Q3 Which organisation runs the World Cup?

Q4 What methods does FIFA use to promote sportsmanship?

ANSWERS

international football contest and the world's largest single-sport event

A1 Jules Rimet

A2 Every 4 years

A3 FIFA (Fédération Internationale de Football Association)

A4 Fair-play awards; all players playing in the World Cup finals and other events are required to sign a fair-play declaration

examiner's note The World Cup is a global event and therefore shares many characteristics with the Olympic Games.

Politics I

Q1 Give three reasons why national governments become involved in sport.

Q2 Why should the UK government want to spend large sums of money on sport in local communities?

Q3 Suggest ways in which the law becomes involved in sport.

Q4 What is meant by social control and how is it significant in the provision of recreation and sport?

ANSWERS

A1 Choose from: economic profit; military preparedness; socialising or nationalising citizens; national prestige; productive workforce; international goodwill; political indoctrination; benefits to individuals

A2 Lower long-term unemployment; lower crime rates; better health; better qualifications; individual and community pride

A3 Negligence; assault; contractual issues; doping issues; equality issues; child protection; event management, etc.

A4 Society seeking to ensure conformity to the dominant norms and values; involving people in sporting activities keeps them 'off the street'

***examiner's* note** Over the last 20 years, sport and politics in the UK have become more closely involved, following a century of keeping them apart. The philosophy of a government towards sport is reflected in the amount and direction of funding.

Politics II

Q1 Why have the Olympic Games often been used as a political tool?

Q2 What is a boycott? Give an example.

Q3 What is the advantage of the British Olympic Association being free from political control?

Q4 Complete the term: 'bread and c.................. theory'. What does it imply about sport?

ANSWERS

A1 They provide a focus for the country hosting the event; worldwide media coverage highlights issues globally

A2 A refusal of a faction to participate in an event in order to deliver a political message; usually a rejection or affirmation of a political regime. A major example was the 1980 boycott of the Moscow Olympic Games, when 52 nations withdrew in protest at Soviet military intervention in Afghanistan

A3 The government can only advise athletes not to attend sporting events

A4 Circuses; it implies that sport can be used by governments to divert the attention of the masses away from problems with the political and social system in which they live

***examiner's* note** Major sporting events require financial support from governments.

Sport and the law

Q1 Why has the number of sport-related prosecutions increased in the last decade?

Q2 State three legal issues that have been associated with sport

Q3 What evidence can you give to suggest that sport and politics have traditionally been kept separate in the UK?

Q4 What was the significance of the case of Jean-Marc Bosman?

ANSWERS

the application of legal principles to all levels of sport and to physical activity

A1 More legislation; more deviant behaviour; people more aware of their rights; attractive compensation; technology used to prove blame

A2 Choose from: racism; sexism; assault; drug taking; hooliganism; corruption; child abuse; personal injury law; contractual law; blood sport laws

A3 Sport organisations traditionally free from political control; no government funding of British Olympic Association

A4 The European Court of Justice recognised that professional sportspeople should enjoy the benefits of the single market and the free movement of workers

***examiner's* note** It is important to recognise that sport is part of society and therefore must be subject to the same rules. If sport did not have to answer to the law, then it would become dysfunctional.

Commercialism

Q1 In what ways can a sports event be commercialised?

Q2 What are some of the disadvantages of commercialism to sport?

Q3 The Mark McKormack Group is an example of a sponsorship agency. What does such an organisation do?

Q4 What is the difference between endorsement and sponsorship?

ANSWERS

an emphasis on the principles of commerce with a focus on profit

A1 Gate receipts; merchandise; catering; advertising; sponsorship/ endorsement

A2 Revenue tends to go to already popular sports; withdrawal of money can lead to a sports event crashing; pressure on performers

A3 Specialises in advising on and organising sports events and programmes; acts as a broker, bringing together the sponsor and sports body to create an event beneficial to both parties

A4 Endorsement: athletes display company logos on equipment and clothing; sponsorship is the provision of funds to an individual/ event for a commercial return

***examiner's* note** Commercialism of sport is related to the prevalent economic system. A capitalist system (e.g. in the USA) is very conducive to commercialism.

Drugs and doping I

Q1 What are anabolic steroids? Why do athletes take them?

Q2 What is meant by blood doping?

Q3 What are beta blockers and in which sports would they be most useful?

Q4 What are stimulants and why would sport performers use them?

ANSWERS

illegal methods of enhancing sporting performance

A1 Artificially produced male hormones; used to build muscle and lean bodyweight and to increase training time

A2 The removal and reinfusion of some of a person's blood in order to increase the number of red blood cells and thereby improve aerobic capacity

A3 Drugs that sport performers might use to steady nerves; useful for activities requiring fine skills, such as shooting

A4 Drugs or similar substances that increase physiological activity; used to improve endurance performance, increase mental and physical alertness, decrease fatigue and increase metabolism

***examiner's* note** You do not need to know about the chemical properties of drugs.

Drugs and doping II

Q1 Suggest four reasons why athletes resort to taking drugs to enhance their performance.

Q2 Why should athletes not take drugs?

Q3 What strategies can organisations implement in order to reduce/stop drug taking in sport?

Q4 What is an ergogenic aid?

ANSWERS

A1 Choose from: enable harder training; build muscle; steady nerves; weight control; fear of failure; rewards are worth the risks; expectations of others; easily accessible

A2 Health risks; disgrace and punishment if caught; it is cheating; dangerous role model for children; potential loss of earnings and sponsorship

A3 Random and out-of-season testing; liaison between organisations; education of athletes and coaches; harsher punishments; more money into testing programmes; use of positive and negative role models

A4 Any substance or object that improves performance

examiner's note As well as knowing the difference between the major drugs, you also need to be able to discuss ethical issues surrounding drugs.

Technology I

Q1 Give three ways in which technology is involved in sport.

Q2 What is HawkEye?

Q3 How can Radio Frequency Identification (RFID) help marathon runners?

Q4 In what way can advance in materials technology lead to conflicts with the sport itself?

ANSWERS

includes the equipment, facilities and sports science that help coaching and training methods, and performance

A1 Choose from: equipment; training; facilities; sports science/medicine; measurement of performance; assistance to referees; media

A2 A sophisticated officiating tool, mainly used in cricket and tennis, which tracks the path of the ball and displays the most statistically likely path

A3 Microchip tracks the runner's time from start to finish and distances in between

A4 Changes the nature of balls or objects (e.g. faster or slower); rackets/clubs can give too much of an advantage; can change the character of a sport

***examiner's* note** It is a good idea to find out more about some of the technology used in certain sports.

Technology II

Q1 What does 'fragmentation of media and sponsorship' mean?

Q2 How can technology help in the preparation of athletes?

Q3 How can technology help fans and audiences?

Q4 What are some possible disadvantages of technology to a sport?

ANSWERS

includes the equipment, facilities and sports science that help coaching and training methods, and performance

A1 People watch video clips on mobiles and online; many more channels to choose from; allows faster and easier global impact

A2 Sport analysis; motion capture; biomechanics; nutrition; rehabilitation; technique improvement; conditioning

A3 Confidence in officials' decisions; intimate knowledge of officials' decisions; wealth of data available (e.g. amount of space covered by a footballer); educated about sports; excitement generated by HawkEye

A4 It can give technologically advanced countries an advantage; conflict between governing bodies and manufacturers (e.g. illegal golf clubs); competitions may be changed to accommodate new technology; it may only be useful in certain sports

***examiner's* note** You need to be able to discuss technology's advantages and disadvantages to the sport, the performer and the spectators.

Hooliganism

Q1 Suggest four factors that might cause hooligan behaviour at a football match.

Q2 Give three prevention and control measures that have been implemented to try to combat hooliganism.

Q3 What theories (other than social class) have been developed to explain hooliganism?

Q4 What is 'deviant behaviour'?

ANSWERS

violent offences occurring in connection with attendance at football matches

A1 Choose from: violence of players; referee's decisions; derby games; alcohol; frustration; diminished responsibility due to being in a large crowd; taunting of rival fans

A2 Choose from: all-seat stadiums; control of alcohol; security checks; CCTV; tougher deterrents; liaison between police departments nationally and internationally; family areas

A3 Hooliganism is a ceremonial system for resolving conflict (Marsh, 1978); psychological deprivation; felt arousal (Elias and Dunning, 1970); political infiltration

A4 Behaviour that goes against society's general norms and values

examiner's note Most exam questions focus on the causes of hooliganism and the strategies implemented to combat the problem.

The media I

Q1 Name three types of media.

Q2 What advantages does media coverage have for sport?

Q3 What is meant by 'globalisation'?

Q4 How can the media reinforce discrimination in wider society?

ANSWERS

forms of mass communication to the general public

A1 Choose from: newspaper/magazine; radio; television; internet

A2 Boosts participation figures; boosts funds; reaches global audiences instantly; provides detailed analysis of an event; can help referees'/umpires' decisions

A3 Increasing interdependencies of societies on a worldwide scale; the mass media draw images from a worldwide arena and transmit them into people's homes through satellite or cable television

A4 Less coverage of female and disabled sport; elite sport focused on more than grass-roots sport

examiner's **note** You need to know the advantages and disadvantages of media coverage for both the sports performer and the sports events.

The media II

Q1 How have the media changed the nature of sporting events?

Q2 How can technology make home viewers feel as though they are at a live event?

Q3 Why should major international sporting events be shown on terrestrial rather than satellite television?

Q4 Suggest two pressures the performer may experience due to extensive media coverage.

ANSWERS

forms of mass communication to the general public

A1 Timing of events has changed; seasons can be extended; increased sponsorship; more participation in sports with greater coverage

A2 Zoom lenses allow close-ups of players; interactive technology follows favourite players; cameras can be set up close to the main action; commentary and crowd sounds bring it to life

A3 Wider audience; national importance; cost of satellite prohibitive to many

A4 Expectations of being a role model; winning is the only important result; intrusion into private life; over-training; playing with injuries; replays can lead to citing after the event

***examiner's* note** You need to understand the relationship between the media and sponsorship, and the control these exert over sport.

Ethics I

Q1 What is 'amateurism'?

Q2 What is 'sportsmanship'?

Q3 Complete the quote from the coach Vince Lombardi: 'Winning isn't the most .... thing, it's the .... thing.'

Q4 How does the Lombardian ethic differ from the code of amateurism?

ANSWERS

the set of moral principles or values held by an individual or group

A1 The ideal that participating in sport should be for the love of it rather than monetary gain, and the participation and effort is deemed more important than winning

A2 Qualities that are highly regarded in sports, e.g. fair play and the observance of the written and unwritten rules of sport

A3 'Winning isn't the most important thing, it's the only thing.'

A4 With the Lombardian ethic, winning is highly valued and there is no honour in losing; in amateurism, taking part is more important than the result — how you participate is more important than whether you win

***examiner's* note** As well as understanding key concepts such as 'amateurism', 'sportsmanship', 'the Lombardian ethic' and so on, you need to be able to compare them and discuss their relevance in the world of sport today.

Ethics II

Q1 What is 'gamesmanship'? Give a sporting example.

Q2 How does professional sport contradict the idea that sport is for leisure?

Q3 Why has sportsmanship declined over the last few decades?

Q4 What are the six Olympic goals?

ANSWERS

the set of moral principles or values held by an individual or group

A1 The art of winning by clever or cunning means without cheating; e.g. a tennis player faking an injury prior to the opposing player serving in order to disrupt the flow of the server's movement pattern

A2 Professional sport becomes the employment/income of the performer and therefore is not carried out in leisure time

A3 Winning has become more important; ethical behaviour in society in general is poorer; pressure from sponsors, coaches etc.

A4 Personal excellence; sport as education; cultural exchange; mass participation; fair play; international understanding

***examiner's* note** The values or ethics of the dominant group in society tend to prevail. The controlling group in the UK would be classed as white, male and middle class. The values of this group have dominated sport over the last two centuries.

Contract to compete

Q1 As well as an agreement to abide by the rules, what else is incorporated in a contract to compete?

Q2 What happens for the contract to compete to be broken?

Q3 Suggest two consequences of repeated breaking of the contract to compete.

Q4 How does the contract to compete differ from the professional sportsperson's contract?

ANSWERS

an unwritten contract to abide by the rules of the sport

A1 All sports performers agree to play as well as they can, allow others to demonstrate their skill and accept the need for codes of behaviour such as fair play

A2 Rules are broken, e.g. a deliberate foul; the performer uses unfair means (e.g. drugs) to give an advantage

A3 Choose from: shame and disgrace to the sport; others discouraged from taking up the sport; harsh penalties, such as bans

A4 The professional contract is a formal, written document

***examiner's* note** Do not confuse the contract to compete with the professional sportsperson's contract.